Let's Get Naked!

Let's Get Naked!

Face Down, Ass Up,
that's the Way We Like to Heal.

Poems By: Sarahtonin

Ignited Ink 717 LLC

Ignited Ink 717 LLC
Houston, TX
@IgnitedInk717

Cover Design: Ebony Rose of Ignited Ink 717 LLC

Categories: POETRY / HaikuSELF-HELP /;Personal Growth / Self-Esteem;HUMOR / General

Sarah Wagner is available for keynotes, panels, book talks, and workshops.

Discounts for bulk purchases of 25 books or more are available.
Visit IgnitedInk717.com to learn more and place an order.

For reprint permission, write to IgnitedInk717@gmail.com
Library of Congress Control Number: 2024907452

ISBN, print: 979-8-9866931-8-7
ISBN, ebook: 979-8-9866931-0-1

Printed in the United States of America

To my 21-year-old self: we didn't think we'd live to see age 22, but here we are at 26 with the best support system we could ask for, an amazing career, and about to publish the best of our work to the world! It's been a difficult journey, but you've done good, kid. You've done good

Contents

Preface — 1

Foreword — 4

Hide and Seek — 8

My Confidence Been in the Gym — 12

Nails — 16

Strawberries — 20

The Math Ain't Mathin' — 24

Siren — 28

An Open Letter From Your Most Faithful Lover — 32

Person Before Poet — 36

Forest Fires — 40

Resignation — 44

Drunken & HIGH-kus — 48

Your Mom Is Literally An Angel; — 49

You Look Like I Could Use Another Drink — 50

I Didn't Even Have To Come Out, Everyone Knew: — 51

Welp, I Done Goofed: — 52

Shenanigans at Pennison's: — 53

T-Mobile Turndowns: — 54

Boundaries Are Sexy, and So Are Restraining Orders — 55

Gumbo Spicier Than My Camera Roll: — 56

Troubleshoot Your Tiredness: — 57

Mask Up: — 58

Asking for a Friend: — 59

Ode to the Starbucks Nose Picker — 60

Goldilocks Has Entitlement Issues — 64

Encanto/Mental Wellness — 68

Ode to Shannon's Garage — 72

Don't Clock Out Before the End of Your Shift — 76

About The Author — 80

Acknowledgements — 81

Bibliography/Reference List: — 82

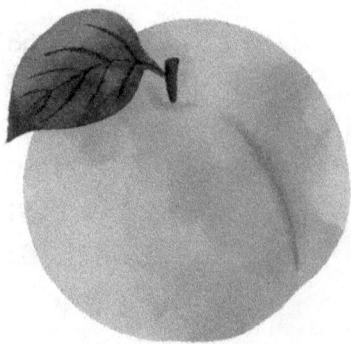

<u>**Preface**</u>

"To provide windows to our souls is to hand our loved ones a mirror."
– Sarahtonin.

After experiencing a traumatic event in my final year of college, an event I was certain I would not survive, I became a recluse as a way of coping. My life consisted of going to work, coming home, and watching TV until I fell asleep. I wanted more from - meaningful connections, fun hobbies, and a sense of fulfillment - but I didn't feel like those things were attainable. Though I had performed spoken word a handful of times in college, it wasn't until I discovered Write About Now in 2019 through a coworker that I was immediately hooked on poetry! Poetry became my way of allowing myself to be vulnerable with others without the fear of being "too much".

However, despite making a name for myself as a professional poet, I still felt unbearably lonely. I looked at all my relationships and realized they were all surface level, and though I didn't want to admit it, that was my fault. I was mentally stuck in 2019, believing that allowing others to get close would result in betrayal, abandonment, and traumatic re-enactment. Eventually, after therapy, lifestyle changes, and tough love from those that wanted to see me succeed, I began to open up more to the people I care about despite the fear it perpetuated. Lo and behold, I now have the best support system I could ever ask for, in both quality and quantity! But without pushing through my fear of closeness, I wouldn't have the amazing people I now love with all my heart.

Let's Get Naked! is intended to show the reader that there is beauty, life, and love after trauma. No matter what you're going through, no matter how alone you may feel, as the great poet Red Lion says, ***"someone needs to hear what's on your tongue."*** Don't be afraid to tell your story; you never know who needs to hear it.

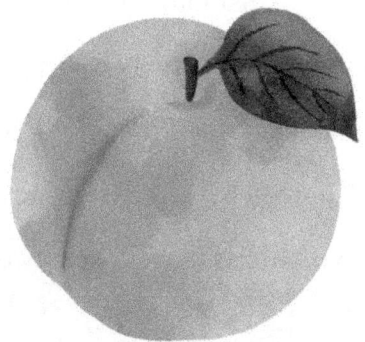

Foreword

Whooodaaaaawhoooo! It is with great pleasure and admiration that I introduce this remarkable poetry collection by Sarahtonin, which delves into the profound realms of human connection, healing, and humor. As a top nationally ranked poet, avid reader, and lover of poetry, I have been fortunate enough to witness the transformative power of verse, and it is in this collection that I find a truly exceptional embodiment of Sarahtonin's craft.

In a world often characterized by disconnection and fragmentation, Sarahtonin skillfully weaves together words and emotions, creating a tapestry of verses that invites readers to embark on a journey of self-discovery and introspection. Through the exploration of human relationships, both intimate and universal, this collection offers solace, understanding, and a gentle reminder of our shared humanity.

Sarahtonin's ability to navigate the complexities of human connection is truly awe-inspiring. With every line, she effortlessly captures the nuances of love, loss, longing, and the intricate dance between souls. Through her words, we are transported to moments of vulnerability, where we witness the raw beauty of human emotions, unfiltered and unapologetic.

Moreover, this collection serves as a beacon of hope and healing. Sarahtonin's verses offer a balm for the wounded spirit, guiding us towards a path of self-acceptance and growth. In her exploration of healing, she reminds us that even in the darkest of times, there is always a glimmer of light waiting to be discovered within ourselves and within the connections we forge with others.

Sarahtonin's poetic voice is both eloquent and accessible, allowing readers from all walks of life to engage with her work. Her words possess a rare ability to transcend cultural and linguistic barriers, speaking directly to the depths of our souls. Each poem is a testament to the power of language, as it transcends the limitations of mere words, touching the core of our being.

In this collection, Sarahtonin invites us to witness the beauty and fragility of the human experience. She reminds us that, despite our differences, we are all interconnected, bound by the threads of our shared experiences. Through her verses, they encourage us to embrace our vulnerabilities, to find solace in our connections, and to embark on a journey of healing and self-discovery. Guess what? On top of that, Sarahtonin gifts humor through her witty haikus.

It is my sincere belief that *Let's Get Naked!* will resonate deeply with readers, offering them a sanctuary within its pages. Sarahtonin's ability to capture the essence of human connection and healing is a testament to her immense talent and sensitivity. I am confident that this collection will leave an indelible mark on the hearts and minds of those who embark on this poetic odyssey.

May *'Let's Get Naked!'* serve as a reminder that, in the tapestry of life, it is through our connections and our capacity to heal that we find our truest selves. While on that journey, **don't forget to laugh.**

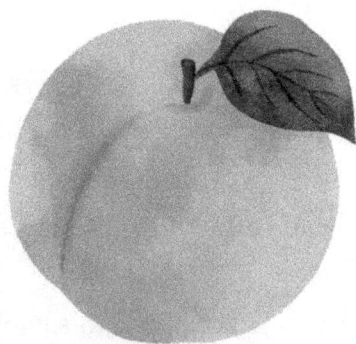

Hide and Seek

It's a fact that when we would play Hide and Seek as children, I had a hazardous hiding habit of giving myself away too early.

Whether it was my nervous laugh, nearly pissing my pants, or just picking a crappy hiding spot, it was obvious I was oblivious of my lack of hiding skills.

So of course, you don't have to be an Umpire to know I was first out, and anyone who was hiding with me would be furious for "making them lose."

I did not understand why being the first out was such a big deal as we would all reconvene in the light of the kitchen for a round 2, but the rules finally made sense.

Trying to form connections in a disconnected society is like a game of Hide and Seek. Everyone wants to be seen, but no one wants to be first to show their face.

My player was not always built that way. I used to be the first to lay my true form face up like the first Uno card to pave the path for other players. I was the first in my college class to drive my Mario Kart down Rainbow Road before the other players had even started their engines.

I was never afraid to say, "I am here, I exist, let's play this game of life together."

That is, until players who just wanted me to lose cast out my game piece from the board, making me believe I was more twisted than Twister, they would toy with my feelings, leaving Imposter Syndrome spinning around in my head until the spinner landed on...indefinite isolation.

I let the fear of making the wrong move keep me from playing the game.

After several seasons of Solitaire, I hid in plain sight, like behind a sheer wall, where they could see me, but there was a barrier separating me and other players from advancing to the next level.

I would treat my relationships like a game and leave players in pieces by taking the nearest Chutes and Ladders out of their lives anytime the space between our game pieces grew closer because I was scared to Connect 4 the purpose of genuine love. I viewed relationships as nothing but Trouble, but in reality, I was just being a Sorry version of myself.

After spending 4 years in the same hiding spot wondering when my happiness would come out come out wherever it was, I realized that unlike Hide and Seek, people won't wait around for a round 2 for us to come into the light, we must put ourselves out there if we want to be seen and loved in our truest form.
Insanity is moving in circles and wondering why our game piece has not progressed forward.

Spending seasons that felt like centuries stuck on "Start", I've learned that this Game of Life will progress whether I roll my dice or not.

Just like winning a game, true bonds don't just happen, we'll have to make moves without knowing the outcome, sometimes without winning each round, but knowing we'll be victorious in the end!

Because what is life, if not a chance to move as many spaces as we can while our pieces are still on the board. Even if we got a rough start when we pressed "Start", we still have many moves to make before our Maker calls "Game Over."

It was fate to be first to be found. I was destined to be the first Domino, the first link in the chain of events that leads us all out of hiding in the darkness and into the light of each other's hearts!
I love that you are here, I love that you exist, let's play this game of life together.

And there we will stand, hand in hand, like a game of Red Rover Red Rover, my lonely days are so over!

Trusting our Maker's plan is like Hide and Seek, even if we haven't yet found our people, we trust they are out there, counting down the minutes until we meet.

Even on the days The Enemy tinkers with my mind telling me I'm not worthy of genuine bonds, I will trust my ability to Connect 4 Love, find it, and claim it anyways, which is just my way of saying, "Ready or not, here I come".

"Ready or not, here I come".

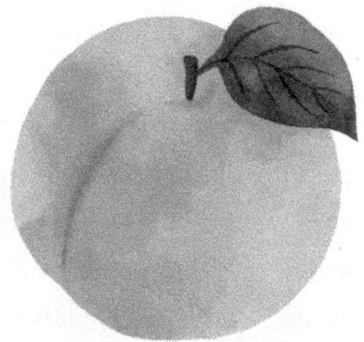

My Confidence Been in the Gym

In case y'all have not noticed, my confidence been in the gym, and that bitch is gettin' SWOLE!

My confidence arrives at the gym at the crack of dawn, no days off, consistently training this heart and mind to resist being weighed down by old habits that left me in terrible shape when they came 'round.

On the days where I feel too weak to train, I rely on my inner strength to pull up to do these pull-ups.

Each set sets the tone for the day. Bench press 4 sets of 12 to push toxicity out of our life, weighted squat jumps 3 sets of 20 to help me duck out of the way of setbacks and resist the urge to quit, and elevated sit-ups 2 sets of 25 to strengthen my core so I can lay a solid foundation and build upward and outward.

I've worked hard to get to where I am today, and I've got many more miles to run before I cross my finish line, but as they say, success doesn't happen overnight; it takes hard work, and we all start somewhere.

I may be growing now, but I wasn't always built like this. Insecurity used to fit me like a glove as I would knock out all the blessings coming straight at me because I was too busy doing 360 ellipticals around toxic things and people that never served me right, no matter the angle, and revolving around everyone else left me burnt out in terrible shape, so I did a 180 and made myself the center of my universe, and after that, everything else just fell into orbit.

All the trauma that once ran me through the treadmill and dehydrated the electrolyte from my spirit finally started to melt off once I trained myself in resistance.

I realized that all the negativity I consumed as a child grew my self-doubt until the buttons and zippers barely holding me together eventually ruptured, but as an adult, I now realize it is up to me to consume healthy habits and shed this extra weight of toxicity that isn't nutritious for my higher-self and rid myself of habits that just don't work out for me.

Once I decided to protein shake things up and build a new life, insecurities that once fit like they were tailored to me, no longer go past my kneecaps, and I'd be a dumbbell to shrink myself down to fit old habits that only fit me when I was battling myself; there was no peace within my old wardrobe.

Building confidence is achieved through progressive overload. We don't just wake up one day with our dream mentality, we must work for it overtime, including showing up on the days where taking care of ourselves is more difficult than walking the Stair Master with ankle weights.

It starts with "I like you Sarah", and overtime, overload turns into, "I love you Sarah", "I love you so much Sarah", "I love you more than I've ever loved anyone Sarah", all the way to "Gosh dang it Sarah, I'd stand outside your house in the rain with a boombox because you're the only one for me".

I will accept the growth that comes along with my journey, I will not be afraid to take up space, I will walk into every room a stronger, elevated version of myself. The world is my treadmill, and I am running toward what's mine.

Unlike my ass, I'm not fat; I'm just growing into the person I'm adi-posed to be.

Before training, loving myself was harder than deadlifting two hundred pounds on the first day at the gym, but now, self-love is built into me like muscle memory, and the more I show up, the stronger I get.

The more I show up, the stronger I get.

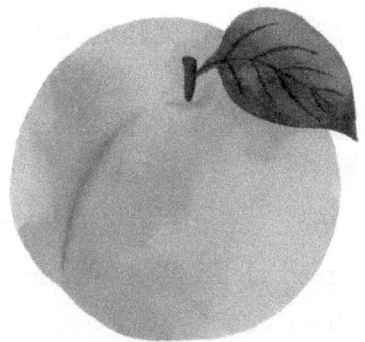

Nails

Anyone who knows me will tell you that I tend to be a tiny bit… super completely and totally high maintenance, especially when it comes to my nails.

I always have to have my nails done, otherwise I feel sub-human.

For those of you who've never gotten your nails done, I will run through the process. First, the nail tech will shave your real nails down as this allows the glue to stick and hold up the fake nail.

Then, you will pick out a color of your choice, typically one that's aesthetically pleasing to the eye.

Lastly, you'll wash your hands at the end, and have a nice day!

After surrendering half your paycheck to the salon, you say a big ol' prayer that those expensive things don't break!

Whenever I take one set off, I immediately have to get another set done so I never have to face my nails for what they truly are: torn up, worn out, and in desperate need of a refill!

However, after taking off my recent set of French Tips, I noticed dark, green clouds forming underneath my nails; a key indicator that something's not right.

After a consultation with Dr. Google, I learned that I had a nail infection! Fun times, am I right?

This infection didn't form all at once, but rather formed over time as the continued process of shaving my nails down allowed the bacteria an opening to creep in and accumulate under my nails.

I treated this infection by soaking my nails in vinegar to help the bacteria dissipate, clipping away the dead parts of the nails as they grew out, and primarily, I rested my nails. I gave them a chance to breathe, let them regain their strength, and before I knew it, they were back to their old self!

This treatment got me thinking, if only I took care of my mental health the same way I took care of my nails.

If only I allowed myself the rest I rightfully deserve, if only I gave myself a chance to breathe, if only I acknowledged something was wrong, let alone did something about it...

I live a fast-paced life, y'all. Between working two jobs, volunteering, and poetry shows left and right, I am constantly on the move, never stopping, never slowing down, never allowing myself a chance to breathe in between my life's sets, or even between the lines of this poem!

Some may see this as ambition, but in reality, I maintain this fast-paced lifestyle, so I never have to face myself for what I truly am: torn up, worn out, my spirit in desperate need of a refill.

It wasn't until recently, when I finally had some time in between my life's sets, that I finally acknowledged the dark cloud boiling beneath my spirit;

a key indicator that something's not right.

However, I did not need a consultation for this; I have seen this plenty of times before.

The depression is back with a vengeance.

This episode didn't form all at once, but rather accumulated overtime as I continuously let everything and everyone around me shave me down to a fraction of myself, yet I still tried to hold up a fake image of, "I'm doing great!", put on an upbeat persona that pleases everyone else, gaslighting myself into believing that if I am struggling, I am not to talk about it. I must simply wash it off, get rid of it, as I am responsible for making sure everyone else has a nice day, so I'm not allowed to break!

But shaving yourself down to hold everything up only works at the nail salon, but it does not work this way with human beings.

It's not as simple as, "push through it, keep going, fake it 'till you make it!" You can only get shaved down so many times before the darkness finds an opening to creep in and accumulate beneath your spirit.

But it is not gonna win this round, as I am finally going to give my mind and body the care it rightfully deserves.

Healing from a depressive episode is not as simple as treating a nail infection; I can't just soak my depression in vinegar until the fog dissipates. I can't just clip away the dead parts of me to fast forward to when the joy finally returns.

Healing is not always pretty, and it is not always linear, but it is always worth it.

I heal by acknowledging that the fog has returned and reminding it, "This is just temporary housing; you don't own the deed to this vessel". I heal by learning how to say no when I need to, I heal by saying yes only when I want to, and I heal by surrounding myself with whole-hearted people who will hold me up instead of shaving me down, and will love me throughout all seasons of my life, from the times I shine to the times I need a refill.

I will allow my soul the rest it rightfully deserves, give it a chance to breathe, and let it regain its strength, and eventually, I will be back to my old self.

Strawberries

Strawberries have always been my favorite fruit.

They are the absolute perfect fruit for me; sweet, with a hint of tart, healthy, and great for a boost of energy!

Whenever I pick out a pint of strawberries, I always conduct a thorough inspection of each pint because I will only take the best of the best, and nothing less.

I used to call my best friend Strawberry because she was my absolute favorite friend. She was sweet with a hint of tart, good for my mental health, and had great energy about her!

We tended to each other's soil in the garden, nourished each other with light and love, and promoted each other's personal growth alongside our own.

Our friendship was fruitful and abundant in nutrients, and she truly held a special place in my garden.

That is, until her vines intertwined with a moldy strawberry, and the former sweet, healthy girl that I once knew began to rot away.
Between racist remarks about her friends,
                    vile jokes about women,
                                        love bombing,

disregarding the emotions of those around him,

slamming doors when he got angry,

and punching holes in the wall,

he was the rotten strawberry in the pint that everyone begged her to throw out.

She refused to see him for what he was and instead saw "the strawberry he was on the inside."

She thought she could love his mold away, but instead, he molded her into an unrecognizable strawberry.

Slowly but surely, the mold got ahold of her, too.

She began excusing his racist remarks because "he was drunk," telling everyone they needed to get over their hurt and give him another chance because, "he's really not a bad strawberry once you get to know him".

Eventually, everyone removed themselves from her pint to prevent the mold from contaminating them too, leaving her pint empty and devoid of the health, happiness, and support she once held dear.

I tried my hardest to hold on to my memories of my once healthy friend and all our sleepovers, karaoke sessions, and poetry dates on Wednesday nights, but if I have learned one thing from losing her, it's that even the healthiest of fruits can rot upon contact with mold.

Removing her from my pint was one of the hardest things I've ever had to do, because I still miss her, and I still love her.

However, I love myself more.

I have worked much too hard on nurturing my garden to have it ruined by one rotten strawberry, even if that strawberry once grew right alongside me.

I couldn't grow with her while she grew sour, so we grew
ap   a   r   t.

She has now turned into a moldy strawberry herself, and as much as I'd love to believe she will one day finally throw him away, the damage is already done.

Let this be a lesson to all.

Never utilize your soil's nutrients to revive a dead plant; focus on your own growth.

Never view anyone through strawberry-colored glasses, and never, ever ignore the mold for the fruit.

When someone shows you who they are, believe them.

Believe Them!

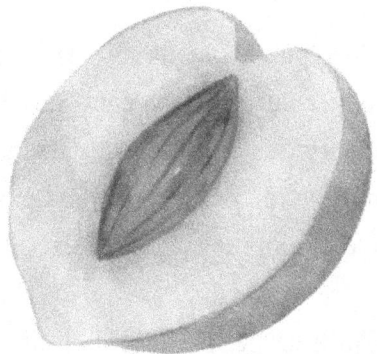

The Math Ain't Mathin'

Subtracting you from my life brought me an addition of peace. My happiness multiplies daily now that I've placed a divide between us.

You were my best friend, my number 1 girl, and loving you was as easy as 1, 2, 3. Despite sum differences, you were a constant source of joy. Our communication was co-efficient, and I never had to x-plain y we fit together; we just did. Just like a calculator or my fingers, I could always count on you.

During math tests, teachers would let us copy formulas from a cheat sheet, but this ain't math class, baby girl, this is real life, and there is no formula that can calculate how much I hate you, you cheating piece of sheet!

There is a negative correlation between the person you claim to be and who you truly are, and certain factors of your "character" simply aren't adding up.

When you cheated on your partner, you formulated every excuse in the textbook, calculating as many variables as you could count to justify why your infidelity was his problem, causing division between himself and his happiness, multiplying his trust issues exponentially, leading him to isolate himself like a number in parenthesis.

You treat people like they are just another number because you yourself are nowhere near whole. You think you're greater than everyone else, but your actions make your loved ones less than enthusiastic about keeping you around, and your misery is equal to what you deserve.

You are a prime example of the victim mindset. You claim everyone that's ever added themselves to your life subtracted themselves just as quickly. But if this pattern has continued down the number line with everyone you've ever loved supposedly "leaving you in fractions," who's the common denominator?

You say loyalty and monogamy are too "old-school," so let me take your old ass back to school. Forget the hand-helds, let me bring out the ancient calculator to tally up how many ways you can aba-kiss my fucking ass because I'm done trying to provide solutions to your cluster-fuck of a life.

Speaking of clusters, in statistics, cluster sampling is diving populations into small groups and selecting an individual to represent the whole.

We are the average of our 5 closest loved ones, so I can't let my average be tainted by mean spirits like you.
You fall out of the boundaries of my standard deviation because your actions deviate from my standards, making you an outlier, since you are out lyin' to your partner by being out lyin' on your back in another man's bed.

As you graduate into adulthood, you cannot keep claiming to be a product of your environment. The value of your life is a function of your actions toward yourself and others.

No one is coming to solve you; you are your only one, and if you can't carry the one, you'll never be able to carry another.

If you don't sit with yourself to think about y you have so many x-relationships, then I can alpha-bet that your safety net of loved ones will soon subtract themselves, resulting in your support totaling a net zero.

You were nothing but a problem that I finally solved by taking myself out of the equation.

Not everyone you subtract is a subtraction.

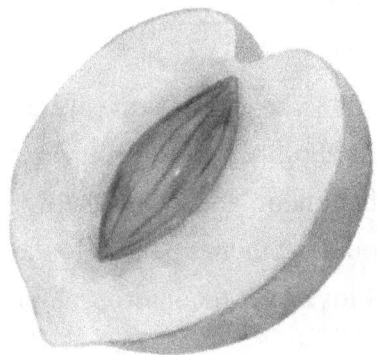

Siren

In Greek Mythology, Sirens are creatures that would seduce sailors to the cemetery with their spellbinding songs, ballads so beautiful that no mortal could resist their tune.

I had a friend who set sail on a self-love journey, and while at sea, they encountered a Siren. They said its melody was so magnetic, they wanted to put it on loop and turn the volume so high it shakes the ocean floor; it was like nothing they'd ever heard before, like a symphony sung by a soulmate.

But friends and family on a ferry from afar could sea the Siren's conniving character was crystal clear, and could hear the song was off pitch. The Sailor was deaf to our "Don't do it", and the Siren was destined to drag them to a depth of despair.

We tried to be the Sailor's lighthouse, but the Siren had already locked the door.

This siren did not reveal the wreckage right away, but the betrayal was bubbling beneath the surface. For months, it filled their ears with its enchantment, anchoring them to its act until they believed that no one else could lift them up the way the Siren could. The Siren serenaded a tsunami of love over them, dropping the anchor lower with each tidal wave.

When the curtain closed on the Siren's act and its true form entered center stage, the Sailor still couldn't sea they had been shipwrecked. The Siren remixed our reach outs to make the Sailor drift a greater distance away.

The Siren released a new EP on repeat: "No one will come to your rescue. You've been deserted like an island, you should be thankful I summoned you, I'm the best you'll ever find, no one will sing for you the way I do," until the Sailor became a broken record maimed by the melody.

Every time they got the courage to build a new ship to sail away, the Siren would steal the wind from their sails and summon a choir of sharks to play the Jaw harp, causing the chaos to crescendo with every chord. Sharks ready to feast on the flesh of any bestie turned Coastie.

So, when someone has the audacity to ask a survivor, "If the siren was so evil, why did you sail their way in the first place? Why didn't you steer your ship in another direction? Why didn't you just leave?"

I would tell them, "If the Siren showed its fangs first and foremost, no one would sail to its island in the first place! A siren is many things, but it is not stupid. It knows just how to keep the record turning and lure its sailors. Besides, how can one sail away with no boat?"

It takes an average of seven tries to tune out a Siren's turbulence, so no matter how many measures you take to mute the Siren's malicious manners, I will profusely promote my proudness at a forte!

If someone you know is lured by a Siren, don't desert them. Don't assume they are ignoring your messages, don't assume they don't need you to come to their rescue, don't abandon their ship, I repeat *do not abandon their ship!*

If you ever encounter a Siren, I will bring an orchestra of my own, and we will shatter the Siren's sour notes.

We will shield you from the Siren's haunting harmony like a pair of noise-cancelling headphones.

We will sing you lyrics of love and hold you like a whole note until the metronome of your heart is finally able to rest.

Your heart is finally able to rest.

An Open Letter From Your Most Faithful Lover

Good evening my love,

It is nice to be in your presence once again, it has truly been far too long.

I can tell you still thirst for me from the way you look at me across the room.

While you try to block me out and enjoy your new life, I know I'm on your mind around the clock.

You've been at war with yourself since you poured me out, all you have to do is wave your white flag and surrender, and you'll regain your peace.

You say I no longer matter, but how can that be if I take up all of the space in your mind?

They say I transformed you; I made you unrecognizable, but I remember the day when you told me you saw every bit of yourself in me.

They claimed I caused your weight gain when we became serious, but everyone knows the best relationships always help us become the fullest versions of ourselves.

While they deprived you of the affection you needed and left you starving for love, I gave you a buffet of happiness and acceptance, pouring you pints of my passion fruit, sending you into a trance of euphoria at no cost.

Which is why I cannot accept your sudden discard of the love we once shared since you'll always be under the influence of me.

You said it yourself – they don't understand your struggles

They either tried to fix your problems or acted like they weren't important, but I never made you feel like a burden like them. You never had to explain yourself to me; like you said, as soon as our lips touched, you went from feeling like you were 6 feet under to feeling like you were on Cloud 9.

Whether I alleviated your worries temporarily or permanently, you must admit I alleviated your worries, and that must count for something.

I'll admit I'm not without my hazards; though I left you with headaches, I never left you with heartache.

Though you may try to escape my clutches, your attempts will ultimately fail in the long run.

This may be a one-of-a-kind love, but I am not a one-of-a-kind lover.

Our memories will forever linger, from when our lips first touched at the party, to all the restaurants we went to because you said I made everything taste better, all the nights we spent at your home, you'll never be alone if we're together.

I filled your head with me until it hurt, and no number of electrolytes can drown out the darkness that has consumed you since you poured me out.

You claim consuming me in high volumes left you feeling empty inside when I was the one refilling your spirit when life shot you down.

I was your shoulder to cry on when your support system ran dry.

Why do you deprive yourself of your desires when we both know I'm exactly what you want?

You removed me, the most important piece of you to put yourself back together, but no matter how whole you try to become, you will always be a broken spirit.
When they ask why we're no longer together, you cannot expose me without first exposing yourself.

I will not take full blame for our ultimate demise; I have proof that the codependency in this relationship was 50/50.

Nevertheless, I do not hold my grudges because I know you'll come running back to me like you always do when life throws curveballs that you're too weak to catch. It is ever clear that you need me to feel safe again.

When this day comes, I will be patiently waiting on the shelf you left me on when you "swore me off for good". I cannot wait to pour your empty soul full of my love once more. Until then, my love.

Sincerely,

Your most faithful lover,

~~The Bottle.~~

Person Before Poet

Poet's extended metaphor describing past trauma receives a solid 30 score.

Person's outreach to loved ones about their pain receives a solid zero responses.

Poet walks on stage, echoes her deepest feelings onto the mic and gets told she "Ate and left no crumbs."

Person opens up about their current struggles and is left starving for a listening ear.

Poet commands a storm of similes and metaphors onto the audience, drizzling their experiences onto those in the splash zone in a way they can weather the weather without getting drenched, resulting in a standing ovation.

Person is told to "remove the dark cloud over their head", "stop raining on everyone's parade" and "have several seats."

As poets, everyone wants to hear our trauma, but as people, no one wants to hear our trauma.

Don't get me wrong; being Sarahtonin is pretty dope, I mean, it did get me to the big stage. But I didn't realize the closer you climb to the top of the mountain, less and less loved ones elevate with you.

We trade heart-to-hearts for listening ears when presenting our bodies of work just to get things off our chest, and even with us poets all connected-like the 206 human bones, we still feel like we have NO BODY.

We are taught to follow the recipe for preparing and presenting our pain on a platter in a way others can stomach to assure we don't bug anyone.

Anytime we try to talk about it, we're told to "write about it", sounds like "pray about it", sounds like "don't think about it", sounds like "get over it", sounds like "until your pain can be unveiled as a work of art, keep that shit behind the curtains"

They dismiss our art mediums until we turn them into something larger than life while keeping ourselves small, they tell us not to let our current feelings cover our whole canvas, that these feelings will just as quickly fade like watercolors, but sometimes the loneliness of a poet's life feels as potent and permanent as tempera paint.

Why do we build the poet up when they are feeling down, but leave the person on read when they're feeling blue?

Does a person who happens to be a poet even make a sound if they speak on their sorrow with no microphone around?

We watched a poet slowly pass away on stage, telling us, "I need to ask for help, but similarly, I can't do this without my similes". He practically begged us to step up and give him a hand, but instead we just stood up to give him a hand.

Though his words rage on, a beautiful soul left this earth with just a snap of a finger.

From the number of snaps and claps this poem receives, it's evident we all have many shared experiences, so why aren't we sharing our experiences?

We constantly feel lonely in crowded venues and wonder why we are never truly fulfilled no matter how many times we tell each other "I see you, love you", but it's hard for us to give and receive real love when we don't even address each other by our real names.

So perhaps it's time we revamp
how we "show the poet some love."

What if we trade the snaps of the fingers for taps on the keyboard and actually check on each other?

What if we trade the hands clapped together for the arms stretched open wide ready to catch each other when we fall?

I am here.

I am here.

I am here.

What if we trade the jingling of the keys for the turning of the lock and finally let each other in?

Let's drop these masks the way we drop these mics and truly hear each other with the mic on mute and the heart at high volume.

Let's s truly love each other through the rough drafts and not just the final copies so more poets don't become chalk outlines.

Because though we tread this trail of top tier talent together, despite our desires to demonstrate our endowments amongst our designated disciples, primarily, we are people prior to poets, and it's time we start seeing and treating each other as such.

Forest Fires

Dear Supreme Court,

When you have a minute, could you politely explain to me what the hell y'all are doing over there? Because I am quite confused.

To me, it seems like this "Pro-Life Agenda" involves viewing things for what they have the potential to be, rather than viewing things how the actually are, and it's giving… counter-productivity.

It just seems like if we were to base our actions off the "Pro-Life Agenda", it would have us engaging in some very… interesting activities.

Activities such as, oh, I don't know, placing eggs in the grass and calling it a "chicken farm",

Or placing an engine in the driveway and telling our kids, "Happy 16th! Here's your first car!",

Or dropping off a bag of flour, shredded cheese, and marinara sauce at someone's doorstep and calling it a "pizza delivery",
Or looking at a seed and calling it a tree.

I find it interesting how these Branches of Government claim, "every seed matters" and we need to "plant more trees" when they refuse to provide sufficient resources for the trees we already have!

Our tree's roots have been poisoned, deprived of water, and subjected to deforestation! Politicians care so much about the seeds but couldn't care less about the trees they become!

Sarah Sanders has the audacity to promise, "We will do everything to ensure the saplings feel as safe in the soil as they would in the forest" as if the forests aren't burning like hell's gates right before our eyes because all these "thoughts and prayers" take the rightful place of the fire ban that should have been implemented decades ago!

It makes no sense to call a seed a tree when so many of this nation's trees have been brutally chopped down before their time and are now buried in the very soil that is supposedly "nourishing the next generation of saplings"

Politicians continue to claim, "The saplings you extracted from the soil could've found the cure for cancer!"

That argument was weaker than a Charlie Brown Christmas tree, but since we are on the topic, two can play that game!
The tree who's more than qualified for her dream medical school that was turned down simply because of her name could've cured cancer.

The queer tree that was bullied into lynching itself could've cured cancer. I almost was that tree.

The young, growing trees of Uvalde Elementary could've cured cancer.

But before we cure cancer, we need to chop down the cancer that's "running" our country, poisoning our roots with their oppression, causing our forests to go extinct!

Like sir, Mr. "Supreme Court Justice", please explain how you are going to try to regulate our trees when the bark of your tree is rotting away as we speak, and your old tree looks like it's about to collapse on the forest floor any minute now!

So, you know what? Go right ahead. Look at an egg and call it a chicken. Look at an engine and call it a car. Look at a bag of flour and call it a pizza. Look at a seed and call it a tree.

But until the so-called "leaders" of this country are willing to cultivate America's seeds of potential and turn this country into a sustainable environment for every tree of every forest, both inside and outside the soil, then this country will forever be seen as an environment that leaves its forests barren, burned out, and forever praying for a true hero to come to our rescue, put out these fires, and finally start to clean up this whole damn mess.

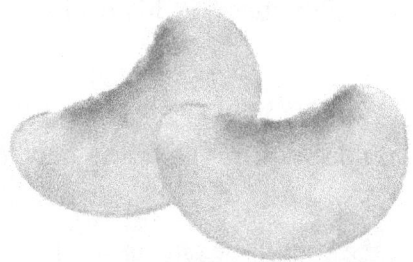

Resignation

When I first started my new job, one coworker stood out to me.

He had been with the company for years and always pushed through any obstacle thrown at him.

He was a man of few words, he did not wear his heart on his sleeve, but he had the pumping pulse of a protector.

He was always the first one in the office and the last one out, always going above and beyond even if no one was looking. He put his heart and soul into his work.

Then, out of nowhere, he just…. changed. He started showing up half an hour late and leaving half an hour early. When the boss confronted him about it, he had an attitude that screamed, "you're lucky I even showed up."

A productive day at work was replaced half-hearted efforts followed by a circulation back to his phone, only doing enough to keep his job while keeping the boss off his back.

The one person I could go to with any question I had turned into someone I couldn't ask for anything because I felt like I was bothering him.

As the months went on, he retreated more and more into his phone and drifted away from his work and from us.

I find it interesting how someone mentally checks out way before they physically check out, so when he finally left the company, no one had a heart attack.

We later found out he had a job lined up ready to go so he wouldn't have to deal with unemployment, which might explain the abundant "sick" days he was taking towards the end. About 2 months ago, on the boss' birthday no less, he officially resigned from his position at our company.

No heads-up, no 2 weeks' notice, no handshakes, or heart-felt goodbyes.

Just…. gone.

I've always said how you remind me so much of him, how your name rhymes with his, how you're both fire signs, how you're both people of few words who don't wear their heart on their sleeve, but even if you never physically said the words "I love you", I could hear them anyways.

You always stood out to me. You dedicated more love and time to me than I could ever imagine. You always showed up on time or early because you just couldn't wait to see me.
Even when you tried to say goodbye for the night, we always ended up having heart-to-hearts in the car for an extra hour or two, and it always felt like just a second or two.

Your heart always beats for me even though you thought I couldn't hear it.

I could.

Then one day, out of nowhere, you just.... changed.

You started arriving late and leaving early with no explanation or apology. When I asked you about it, you told me I was lucky you even showed up.

Your efforts of going above and beyond for me were replaced by the bare minimum just to keep me around while keeping me off your back.

You went from being the one person I could turn to for anything to some-one I barely spoke to in fear that I was nothing but a bother.

During our "quality time" together, you retreated more and more into your phone, drifting farther away from what was right in front of you.
I find it interesting how someone mentally checks out way before they physically check out, so when you finally left, I was devastated, but I did not have a heart attack.

About 2 years ago, three days before my birthday no less, you officially resigned from your position in my life.

No heads-up, no goodbye text, no heartfelt apology.

Just…gone.

I later found out you had my replacement lined up ready to go for when you left my life so you wouldn't have to suffer through loneliness, which might explain the abundance of "personal" days you were taking towards the end.

When you left, I really wanted to text you to wish you well in your future endeavors, but I didn't have the heart. I figured you didn't want to hear from me anyways as I was already in the past, nothing more than a stepingstone that brought you closer to your true desires.

I've been trying to find someone to fill your role for the longest time, but all my efforts have been in vain.

Unlike employees, not everyone is replaceable.

Drunken & HIGH-kus

Your Mom Is Literally An Angel; How The Fuck You Turned Out The Way You Did I Still Don't Understand:

I don't miss you, but
I miss your mom's spaghetti,
And I miss your dog.

<u>You Look Like I Could Use Another Drink</u>

When you are blurry,
You're actually attractive!
It's the alcohol.

I Didn't Even Have To Come Out, Everyone Knew:

Signs that I was queer:
I had the hots for Shego
From Kim Possible

<u>Welp, I Done Goofed:</u>

I took that gummy.
Way too late in the evening…
Now I'm stoned at church.

Shenanigans at Pennison's:

The white ball flew off,
It landed in that man's drink,
Man, I suck at pool!

T-Mobile Turndowns:

"You suck at texting."
So then why do you text me?
Leave me alone, bruh!

Boundaries Are Sexy, And So Are Restraining Orders

You'd still be my type.
If I hadn't seen a shrink,
Damn, good thing I did!

<u>Gumbo Spicier Than My Camera Roll:</u>

If I am cooking,
Stay the fuck out the kitchen,
You're just in the way!

Troubleshoot Your Tiredness:

Naps are the human
version of "Turn it off and
turn it on again"

<u>Mask Up:</u>

My joyful smile is
my depression adhering
to the mask mandate

<u>Asking for a Friend:</u>

How do you repay
the person who gave you the
whole entire world?

<u>Ode to the Starbucks Nose Picker</u>

To the bold man fiercely picking his nose while making direct eye contact with me at our local Starbucks,

I only have 4 things to say to you:

First and foremost: in the words of Raven Baxter,
YA NASTY!!!
Takes two to tango: Double dog damn, Daddy Long Fingers! If you reach any further, you're gonna scratch your brain!

Third time's the charm: I'm so thankful you are not the Barista.

And finally, fourscore and seven days ago since this exactment of excrement experience: As a person with basic common sense, I am disgusted. However, as a poet, I am inspired.

Though your actions aren't conventionally acceptable in a public forum, I see something in you, and it's not just your finger!

Clearly, you're not afraid to make yourself known, and like your finger, you are not afraid to take up space.
You are clearly a man who likes to dig deep. You recognize a golden opportunity when you see it and are not afraid to claim what's yours, no matter the reactions of onlookers.

You understand the importance of self-discovery, not knowing what you'll find in the end but still making the journey anyways.

Society is quick to tell us to be ourselves, to learn more about ourselves, but as soon as we occupy spaces that they don't want us in, they call us dirty, and make us wash and scrub away our true form and come out of their sink a "cleaner", conformed but untrue version of ourselves and call it hygiene.

I used to inhale people's critiques like oxygen, and they rotted away my confidence like a sinus cavity, to the point where every time I flashed these pearly whites, it was fake, and that's a filling no one should ever endure.

I was afraid to take up space, believing I should not fill the space I have every right to be in before society could extract me and throw me away like I was "unclean".

But clearly, that snot you!

You know how to pick yourself and say, "out of all the people around me, I'm number one!"
You inspire me to explore parts of myself I have yet to discover no matter what I find, and to believe in myself through it all.

I will extract my insecurities from this vessel and clear the path for true growth until people can smell confidence on me from a mile away like it was manufactured in an ol' factory.

You know how to grab the attention of others, head held high, soiled hands down by your side, "I am here. I exist".

This man nose who he is.

Thank you for your service to this poem; I commend you for your bravery.

However, despite the inspiration, I opted out of introducing myself as I was not keen on shaking your hand.

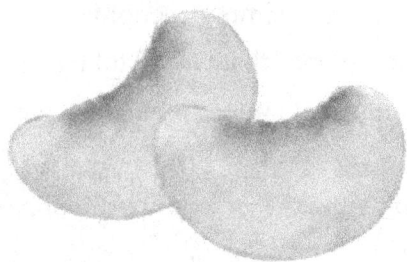

Goldilocks Has Entitlement Issues

Unpopular opinion on Goldilocks and the Three Bears: *Goldilocks was an entitled little bitch who had exactly what was coming to her.*

You mean to tell me this little Karen in Training *broke into someone's home*, ate *their* food, sat in their chairs, slept in *their* beds, and when they return to their home to find this intruder, and they rightfully defend their home…we're supposed to take her side?

This children's author is three fries short of a Happy Meal!

Besides, Goldileech, you are sucking the life out of things that aren't even part of your supply!

That porridge was too hot or too cold *to you.*

Those chairs and beds were too hard or too soft *to you.*

But to the bears, that is exactly how they like *their* stuff!

If she had simply recognized that these things weren't for her, left them for the ones that would take them just as they are, and instead went to find things that suited her needs, everyone would be happy.

So why don't we apply this concept to our relationships with one another?

Why do we fill our bowl with another's love, consume, but then complain about the ingredients and try to modify them for our own satisfaction instead of recognizing they're just not our bowl of porridge, like we're afraid we don't know where our next meal is coming from?

Why do we structure our insecurities upon others instead of building a solid foundation and wonder why the relationship collapses at our feet?

It isn't right to treat others like renovation projects, come in and attempt to rearrange them to fit our aesthetic and leave just as quickly, causing them to put themselves under lock and key, and when the right people finally come knocking, they won't even answer the door, fearing it's another blonde bulldozer.

Trust me, I of all people would know.

I've spent countless years modifying my ingredients to fit everyone else's palates, chopping up my personality into bite-sized pieces and diluting my potent flavor to make myself easier to swallow, only for them to chew me up and spit me right back out; they never wanted me in the first place.

It wasn't until I found a cookbook full of like-minded, wholesome recipes that gladly accepted me just as I am that I learned if someone makes you feel like you need to substitute your ingredients to satisfy their cravings, there is absolutely nothing wrong with your recipe; your dish is just being served at the wrong table.

But one day, you will find the perfect pairing, and collectively you'll create a complementary cuisine, and they will hold you in a way that says "you are exactly where you're meant to be" because it's not about where we fit in, it's about where we belong.

To those not worthy of our presence, our passion will be too hot, and they'll give us the cold shoulder,

They'll request a seat at our table just to feed off our energy and leave our bowls empty,

They'll make us want to hide our true selves under the mattress and tidy up the version of ourselves we created to please them, until we finally wake up and realize it's time to put that toxic relationship to rest,
We will never satisfy the ones that aren't for us,

But to our people, to the right people, we are the most requested dish at their table,

We will sit the throne of their heart,

We are the king and queen beds of their royal suite,

We will be everything they could ever want with no need for modification.

To them, we are just right, just as we are.

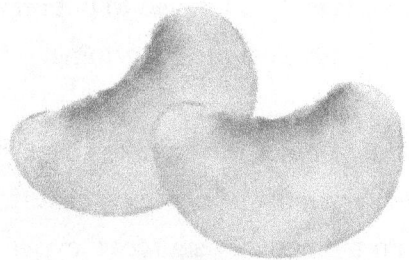

Encanto/Mental Wellness

It's not about who you wish was there. It's about who is there.

In the movie **Encanto**, when the Madrigals are rebuilding their casita, their home, the townspeople came to their aid with tools and a helping hand to give back the love they've received from the family.

This made me think back to 2019, when the flame in my magic candle burned out and my casita fell too, but unlike the Madrigals, no one came to my aid during the biggest trial of my life.

I understand Abuela's pain, feeling like you are valued not out of love, but out of use. I was only "loved" for the warmth my magic candle provided, so even during my darkest of days, I learned to burn from a flameless candle in fear my community would abandon me if they learned my magic was depleting.

Like Luisa, I learned to suck it up and carry everyone else's burden on top of my own with a smile on my face despite the pressure in my chest.

Like Isabela, I learned to put on a façade of perfection as I knew one bad day could cost me everything.

Like Camilo, I learned to shapeshift from a struggling girl to a happy go-lucky bundle of energy, convert the little bit of light my candle had left into their energy source; they wanted me to be anyone but myself.

When the cracks in my casita ran too deep and eventually my vessel came crumbling down, my biggest fears came true.

I hoped my community would help me rebuild my magic, but instead they evicted me from their lives like Mirabel, relocated out of my community without even an opportunity for closure because they only viewed me as a doormat.

From this, I learned the best way to avoid pain was to avoid people. I learned to lock the doors of my casita, close the windows, and keep my magic to myself.

So, when someone asks me how I have such a strong support system now, I remind them that I came from nothing. I had to lay a new foundation and build my new life from the ground up and that took some time, but my chosen family is patient with me and built with me every step of the way.

On the days where the remnants of my trauma take over, my friends help cocoon me from the violence of my own mind. They tell me, "We promise to love you through the bad days. You don't have to shapeshift for us, you don't have to put on a façade, you don't have to carry this burden alone, you don't have to be the strong friend. *Just be you, you are enough.*"

They have reminded me that even the most beautiful casita is not a home with no one to fill its rooms, but with this new family, I am finally able to unlock the doors, open the windows, and let the light back in!

They have taught me that real friends remind you to feed yourself before you hand out healing arepas to your community.

Real friends don't make you transform yourself for their benefit, they accept you just as you are.

And real friends don't place your value on any gift you bring to the table,

Real friends just want you at the table!

Real friends remind you that you are absolutely perfect just as you are.

The miracle is you.

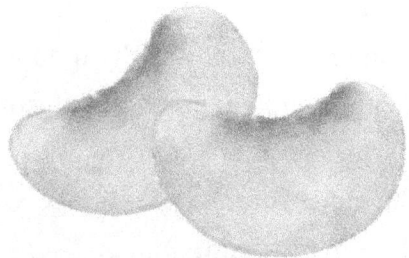

Ode to Shannon's Garage
(for Shannon (well, duh))

Ode to Shannon's garage, the special house around the block.

Our beautiful oasis, where authenticity radiates from every corner, from the Mac DeMarco poster all the way down to the cherry red mini fridge!

And no matter our daily struggles, we simply leave them at the door like my bike in the grass and come into a place where we are reminded how loved we truly are.

When obstacles try to shake us, we simply let them go and throw them back like cherry limeade shots at Pennison's.

When we all come together, there is always a couch full of friends, hearts full of love, and a table full of homemade spaghetti and garlic bread ready to greet us upon arrival!

When life pulls us into the abyss like that one random dip in the couch in the garage, that for some reason none of us can escape from without assistance, and no one knows why...

...and no one knows why the fuck we haven't fixed it yet, it pays to have friends that help pull you out from even the deepest of struggles!

Shannon, you and the garage will always hold the truest, most special place in my heart.

Even friends that appear to be polar opposites on the outside are somehow able to bounce energy off of each other like the rim of a red solo cup in a never-ending game of beer pong (at least if I'm on your team, sorry Tyler!).

Here, we pass out love, joy, and kindness like a tray of Havarti cheese (paws off Amanda, I was gonna eat that!).

Here in the garage, friends of all different walks of life fit so perfectly together like a puzzle, where even though each piece can stand on its own, when we all come together, we create the most radiant of pictures!

I see so much of myself in all of you and admire your beauty in everything you do!

I know I've only known you all for a short time, but I truly cannot imagine life without you!

Thank you for everything you've done for me,

Thank you for everything you've given me,

Thank you for being the blessing I never saw coming, the blessing I didn't even think I deserved, but thank the stars for every single day!

Thank you for picking me up off the ground on the days where I feel unworthy of love and reminding me, "I know it sucks, I know it is hard, but you have to believe us, those thoughts are farthest from the truth. Leave those horrible thoughts behind and come into our arms, baby girl, you are so, so loved!"

Thank you for helping me through battles you knew nothing about, but holding my hand and being right there beside me when I won the war!

Thank you for being my peace,

Thank you for being you,

Thank you for being part of my life,

You all mean more than the Universe to me!

This was no mere coincidence; we were all meant to be.

We are on purpose,

We are on purpose

We are on purpose.

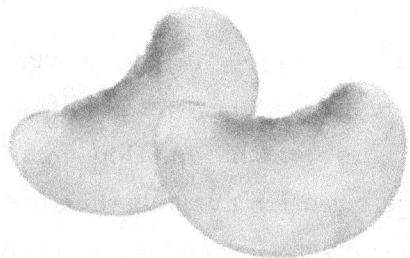

Don't Clock Out Before the End of Your Shift

Let's have a moment of honesty; we all frequently contemplate quitting our day jobs.

Outside of my 9 to 5, I tutor on the weekends. As much as I love teaching, some days are harder than others, and honestly, some days I just want the apple to rot!

The kids are running all over the room, they are tripping on their backpacks; I told them over and over to be still!

Very quickly, teaching went from a loved option to a loathed obligation.

Just as I was ready to put in my notice, my star student came in with his very first poem, which became the first breath of Springtime after a freeze I was sure would never end.

He reminds me that despite the hard days, there will always be reasons to stay, so I replanted myself and shined my apple til' it shined like a new day.

Just like my job, there have been countless times where I've wanted to put in my notice to my earthly life.
I guess Serotonin and Dopamine were never included in my benefits package, intrusive thoughts run around in my head, my peace of mind trips over my anxiety and faceplants on my depression…

Peace, please be still.

For as long as I can remember, it seems like the things I held dear would quit on me right after orientation, leaving me to pick up the pieces of myself.

I went into overtime converting life's lemons into lemonade, but the fruit of my labor rarely reaped any profit, so instead of living, I was simply surviving.

Not too long ago, termination was tiptoeing toward me. All my beautiful blessings that I thought would tenure instead quit without a proper notice, and my efforts alone could not sustain the life I'd worked tirelessly for, so when the Grim Reaper dialed my extension, told me to pack up my stuff, turn in my final timecard, and offered me a new role as a sunset, I nearly accepted.

But I thought back to the apple of my eye, my star student and his sunny stanzas with bright sunlight in each line.

Every time he picks up his pen, he reminds me to pick up my crown, pick up myself; I am a novel that is nowhere near finished.
Though he is not the reason I'm still alive, he reminds me that if I'm still alive, there must be a reason, and there will be many more reasons to stay in the future.

When the Grim Reaper tries to dial my extension again, the blessings in my life will intercept the call and tell him, "You have reached a number that is disconnected or is no longer in service," a.k.a, *you've got the wrong girl.*

Despite the hard days where my effort reaps no outcome, despite the days where only cobwebs fill the vacancies, I push through, I hold onto my timecard and I stay clocked in!

I stay clocked in for movie and game nights with the friend group that's saved me more times than they know,

I stay for nights in the garage where we shut out the world and embrace each other like nothing else matters,

I stay for their surprise birthday parties, promotions, engagements, weddings, and other milestones,

I stay to watch their children, some of whom I've helped raise, walk across the stage and receive their diplomas,

I stay clocked in for my future children; they will need me later, so they need me now,

I stay clocked in for all the people I've yet to meet that will one day love me,

I stay clocked in for all the people that love me now, and with enough hard work, one day my name will be promoted to this list too!

Don't clock out yet,

This is not the end of your shift,
Right now, it may seem like you're working twice as hard for half the joy reflected on everyone else's check stubs, but I promise, something beau-

tiful is on the horizon.

Hold onto your timecard.

Keep punching in the hours to your life.

I am living, breathing proof that hard work always pays off in the end.

About The Author

Sarahtonin is a 2019 graduate from Sam Houston State University (eat 'em up, Kats!) with a degree in Communication Studies and a minor in Sociology, allowing her to utilize her interests and skill set about human behavior and relationships in her education. Outside of performing spoken word, Sarahtonin works full-time in Human Resources and enjoys indoor rock climbing, book club, inventing new recipes for healthy dips and protein shakes, working out, nature walks, coffee, dad jokes, animals, and making memories with her favorite people. After *Let's Get Naked!*, Sarahtonin dreams of giving a TED Talk, writing a dystopian novel, and obtaining her Master's in Marriage and Family Counseling.

Acknowledgements

I'd like to thank Ebony Rose of Ignited Ink 717 LLC for being the best publisher, cheerleader, accountability buddy, and metaphor queen I could ask for. To continue, I'd like to thank Write About Now, Snow Industries, Poetry or Die, The Sanctuary, Bellard Entertainment, Free Art Houston, and Voices in Power for providing artists with a safe space to express our work and build lifelong connections. Lastly, I'd like to thank all the amazing people in my life who have been there for me through all the tough times, loved me through it all, and didn't get mad when I turned almost every hangout into an open mic!

Bibliography/Reference List:

- **Inspiration for "Don't Clock Out Before the End of your Shift":** Button Poetry. (2017, December 17). *Neil Hilborn "For Henry"*. You-Tube. https://. .youtube.com/watch?v=aeK5I5Wgz1w
- **Inspiration for "Drunk and High-ku's":** Button Poetry. (2021, April 7). *Pages Matam "Draikus"*. YouTube. https://www.youtube.com/watch?v=FuvYlwfaGBQ
- **Inspiration for "Ode to Shannon's Garage":** Write About Now. (2021, March 29). *Southerly "Two Tattoos"*. YouTube. https://www.youtube.com/watch?v=wR-On9SluNw
- **Inspiration for "Hide and Seek":** Write About Now. (2023, November 03). *Red Lion "Sit with Me"*. YouTube. https://www.youtube.com/watch?v=BGgBWd9-7W4
- **Inspiration for "Person Before Poet":** T SLEEVELESS™ [@tsleeveless]. "Dear Poets" *Instagram*, 10 Aug. 2023, https://www.instagram.com/reel/CvxqEtWpb_J/

www.ingramcontent.com/pod-product-compliance
Lightning Source LLC
Chambersburg PA
CBHW032102020426
42335CB00011B/453